Our Earth

Written by Jane Calame
Illustrated by Daniela Frongia

atmosphere press

This book is dedicated to my family, friends, the current children of the world, and the future generations yet to grace us with their presence. May you all find health, happiness, and harmony in this life.

So you've been born! Welcome, Hooray! The people are glad you made it to Earth today.

There are cities
and towns
and some places wild.
You may live in any of these
little mystical child.

But no matter where you live,
some things must be done
To care for this planet, as we have only one.

You'll grow,
you'll learn, and
live on this planet.
So here are some tips to
help you befriend and protect it.

Do your best to save water,
our most precious resource.
How? When not in use,
turn off the faucet of course!

Feel a chill at home? Forget the thermostat.
Layering on a sweater will take care of that!

And when leaving a room,
remember to turn off the light.
If you're not there in it,
it need not be bright.

Compost!
Recycle!
Use only what you need.
Keeping our waste minimal
helps the planet succeed.

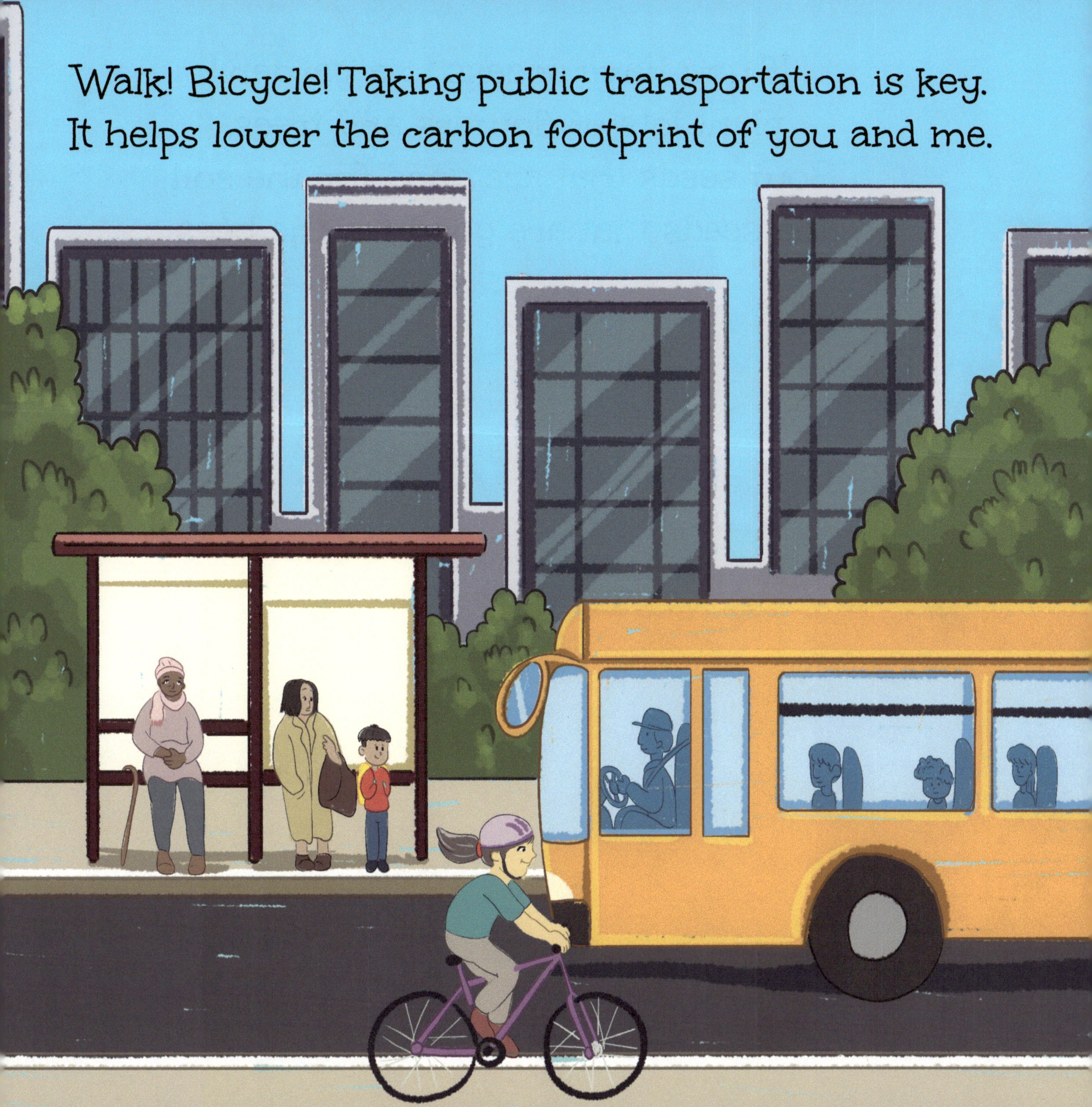
Walk! Bicycle! Taking public transportation is key.
It helps lower the carbon footprint of you and me.

If you have access to a garden,
plant lots of flowers and trees.
Sow seeds that are good for the soil
and seeds that are good for the bees.

Bees pollinate flowers, giving us

and

Good for your eyesight
and building strong bodies.
Helping you grow. Thrive! Succeed!
FINISH

Taking care of our planet is a delicate art,
But everyone is a hero when doing their part.

Because without the art of participation
our Earth is just, eh....
So go out there, little one,
and save the day!

About the Author

Jane Calame is a childcare professional with almost 20 years experience in the field. She is presently working as a PreKindergarten teacher in her native city of San Francisco. The daughter of two environmentalists, sustainability and the natural world have been her passions from an early age. As an educator she hopes to teach and inspire future generations to live with an eco conscious mindset as well. In her free time Jane enjoys: gardening, hiking, biking, taking the bus to museums, lounging around with her two cats, drinking tea, and playing Scrabble with her family.

About the Illustrator

Daniela Frongia, also known as Caisarts, was born in Sardinia, Italy and is a digital illustrator with more than 10 years of professional experience. Since she was 5 she grew up drawing Disney characters until she discovered the anime world. She graduated from Art School and after various art work experiences, decided to move to London, where she had her first personal art exhibition. Later she discovered the digital world, which gave her more flexibility, as she loves to travel. She enjoys working in a vast variety of artistic branches including children's books illustration, book cover artwork, greeting cards, and character design. During past years she has been lucky enough to work with great authors, book publishers, as well as a big animation studio as character designer.

About Atmosphere Press

Atmosphere Press is an independent, full-service publisher for excellent books in all genres and for all audiences. Learn more about what we do at atmospherepress.com.

We encourage you to check out some of Atmosphere's latest releases, which are available at Amazon.com and via order from your local bookstore:

Alley: I Have Albinism, by Alethea Allen
Santa on a Surfboard, by Laura Sharp
Lilah Loves Life, by Brian Sullivan
The Christmas Witch, by Jaime Katusha
My Sister is Sick...What About Me?, by Mary Kay and Eli Olson
There's a Spider in My Bed, by Devon Nunnally and Biaina Alexanian
Yikes, I Saw a Barracuda!, by Tamara Anderson
Winston's Big Wind, by Barbara Reyelts
Finnigan the Finicky Donkey, by Ashley Vail
Holidays in Trees: Harvest Festival, by Cammy Marble
I Have Worry Monsters in My Tummy, by Erica Wilson, M.ED., LPC., NCC
The Tail of a Trio, by Katherine Scott
Cow Days, by Christina Warfel
Logan and Lexi Meditate, by Denesia D. Rogers